Crops on the Farm

by Teddy Borth

capstone

ABDO
ON THE FARM
Kids

Photo Credits: Shutterstock, Thinkstock

Production Contributors: Teddy Borth, Jennie Forsberg, Grace Hansen
Design Contributors: Dorothy Toth, Laura Rask

Library of Congress Cataloging-in-Publication data is available on the Library of Congress Website.
ISBN 978-1-4966-1002-7 (paperback)

Printed and bound in the USA.
009942F16

Table of Contents

Crops on the Farm 4

Corn 6

Wheat 10

Cotton 14

Oranges 18

More Facts 22

Glossary 23

Index 24

Crops on the Farm

Farmers grow **goods** on the farm. These goods are called crops. United States farmers grow many crops.

4

Corn

Farmers in Minnesota grow corn. Corn plants grow very tall!

7

People eat corn. Farm
animals eat corn too!

Wheat

Farmers in North Dakota grow **wheat**. Wheat looks like tall grass.

Wheat is in food. Bread

is made with wheat.

12

Cotton

Farmers in Georgia grow cotton. Cotton is white and fluffy.

14

Cotton is soft. Cotton is used in clothes. Cotton is in towels.

Oranges

Farmers in California
grow oranges. Oranges
grow on trees.

Oranges are round. Oranges are **squeezed** to make juice.

More Facts

- Corn is the most popular crop in the United States.

- Corn has more uses than any other crop. It can be used in making cooking oil, sugar, plastics, glue, fuel, and more!

- What farmers can grow depends on weather and soil.

- The average farm is about 1 square mile (2.5 sq km), which can hold 484 football fields.

Glossary

goods – produce from the farm that is traded for money.

squeeze – to press together tightly.

wheat – a plant that is grown and turned into flour. Flour is used to make breads, cereals, cakes, and more.

Index

animals 8

bread 12

California 18

clothes 16

corn 6, 8

cotton 14, 16

farmer 4, 6, 10, 14, 18

Georgia 14

juice 20

Minnesota 6

North Dakota 10

oranges 18, 20

United States 4

wheat 10, 12